INFORMATION SECURITY LEADERS HANDBOOK

HOW TO BE AN EFFECTIVE INFORMATION SECURITY LEADER

BY

FOCUSING ON FUNDAMENTAL MODELS

RAFEEQ UR REHMAN

Downloads

There are frequent changes to this material on a quarterly basis. Please visit web site http://InfoSecLeadersHandbook.wordpress.com for updates.

Table of Contents

1 Preface - Ready, Set, Go!

The information security threat landscape changes frequently as a result of changes in technologies, economic issues, globalization, social activism and hectavism, new political realities, and innovations by plain old criminals who want to steal data for financial benefits. Along with, the role and responsibilities of security professionals, especially the ones in the leadership roles, also change. Instead of playing a catch up game all the time, this book emphasizes focusing on basic principles and techniques. The information security leaders should implement these principles to update their personal knowledge, to safeguard their organization's information assets and optimize information security cost.

After having meetings with many information security leaders in diverse industry sectors, I have realized that there is a set of "fundamental" models and approaches that help these leaders run successful and effective information security programs. This book is a summary of these fundamentals.

Who are the target audience?

If you are an information security professional, whether in a leadership role or aspiring to be a future leader, this book is for you.

What is this book about?

The objective of this book is to make you successful as information security professional by learning from experience of great leaders in this field. It provides core fundamental models in a concise manner that are easy to read and use in managing information security. Most of the chapters accompany visual mind maps, action items, and other visual tools for easy understanding.

How is this book organized?

The book covers a set of carefully selected topics. This is to ensure that focus remains on principles that are the most important to the success of a security professional. The topics are arranged in six parts as listed below.

1. **Know The Business** – List of topics important for understanding and knowing the business.

2. **Information Security Strategy** – Elements of information security strategy, how to create strategy and put it into practice.

3. **Security Operations** – Major areas related to running an effective security operations program.

4. **Risk Management** – How to assess and manage risk.

5. **Personal Branding** – Creating personal brand and establishing credibility to be effective as information security leader.

6. **Appendices** – Miscellaneous data points and sources of information.

How I Use This Book?

I suggest you read one chapter daily, take actions, set goals, and write those actions and goals on the "**Goals and Activity Log**" page at the end of each chapter. Next day, read another chapter and write the actions and goals with target dates. As you go along, start reading random chapters and keep on reviewing and updating your actions and goals to measure your progress and success.

A Systematic Way of Achieving Excellence

The book provides a systematic and measureable way towards excellence in your job. I have gone to great length to limit each topic to two pages or less. Please use the "**Goals and Activity Log**" page to record your progress and make the best use of your time. While you go along, record your experiences and share them on the book web site.

Book Web Site

Many detailed mind maps, new articles, and discussions are made available at the book web site http://InfoSecLeadersHandbook.wordpress.com. New content will be added on an ongoing basis and you can actually publish your own mind maps on this web site. I would like this web site to be driven by the community where you can share your experiences, tools, mind maps, and any other information to help the information security leaders. Please register on the web site to receive updates.

Acknowledgements

I am thankful to all of my friends who shared their thoughts and gave feedback to prepare manuscript. Ruth Reiss has been very helpful in reviewing the manuscript and ensuring the readers can easily understand it.

Questions, Comments, Criticism, Appreciations

Please contact the Author, Rafeeq U. Rehman, at rafeeq.rehman@gmail.com for any questions or comments or provide any feedback that can be helpful in the next version of this document. All types of critique are welcomed, as long as it is short!

Rafeeq U. Rehman

PART ONE

Know The Business

2 Using Mind Maps and Other Visual Tools

Great communication is key to success for great leaders. Great communications does not mean lengthy documents and hundred page long PowerPoint presentations. There are many new tools that convey messages more effectively and Mind Map is one of these. Embrace these new tools.

- Use **Mind Maps** for describing security initiatives and their relationships in a bigger picture.

- You can also use **Infographics** for education and awareness.

Mind maps are great visual tool to understand, as well as convey, relationship among different activities. You will find many mind maps throughout this book as visual depictions. I use a software package "XMind" to draw mind maps. However, you don't need to purchase a mind mapping software. Hand drawn mind maps are just fine. As of writing of this book, a free version of XMind with limited options is available for download. I encourage you to draw mind maps by hand while using this book as well as in your daily life.

The first mind map shows this book sections. In fact I have used mind maps to draw a detailed outline and table of contents of this book under each of these sections.

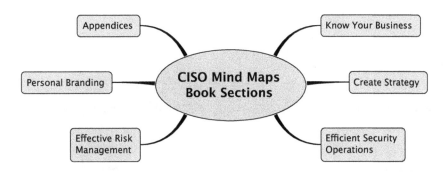

You can use mind maps to create your weekly schedule, TODO list, learning new things, goals and objectives, and many other things. As the complexity and inter-relationships of information security operations grows, you will find mind maps are very effective tool not only to understand these complexities but to communicate to others as well.

A little practice with mind maps in the start of this book will be very useful. As suggested earlier, use of paper and pen for creating mind maps is sufficient.

SUGGESTED ACTIONS

On the next empty page, draw mind maps for the following as an exercise.

- **Organizational Chart** – A mind map of CIO organizational chart with CIO in the center of the mind map.

- **Business Structure** – A mind map of major departments in your organization.

- **Personal Goals** – A mind map of your personal goals for this year, or event quarterly and monthly goals.

- **Income/Expense** – Create a mind map to show major income and expense sources of your company's business.

- **Info Security Tasks** – Create a Mind Map showing everything that information security does. You can take it to your board or leadership meetings to give them a quick overview of your contributions.

- **Presentations** – Consider using a Mind Map in your next presentation.

- **Templates** – Make Mind Maps integral part of information security documents and templates.

- Create a new Mind Map every month and publish it on your internal or external blog.

- **Standardize a Mind Mapping Tool** like XMind of FreeMind (or any other tool you like).

As you may have realized by now, you are also learning your company's business while drawing these mind maps. Don't worry about completeness of these mind maps at this point. As you build better understanding of the business, you can modify these mind maps later on.

CREATE SAMPLE MIND MAPS

Use this page to practice creating mind maps listed on the previous page

3 Learn Your Organization's Business

The primary reason of existence of any business is to make money. The reason for existence of information security team in an organization is to effectively manage the business risk related to information security. Any great CISO (or a person in a leadership position) must understand how the organization's business works. Note that I am using "*business*" as a loose term. In case of government organizations, the *business* may be providing certain services to your constituents. The key thing to understand is that every organization has a purpose and the information security has to support that purpose. The only exceptions to this are the vendors of information security products and services where information security itself is the primary business. So unless you are working for an information security company, the primary business of your organization is something other than information security and you must understand it thoroughly.

Learning business boils down to only two things:

- How your organization earns money?
- Where the money is spent?

The corporate strategy and organizational structure controls these two major objectives. As an information security professional, the more you understand company's business, the more effective you will be to put information security in the context.

SUGGESTED ACTIONS

Following is a list of basic information that you should know about the business of your organization.

- **Organizational Structure** – Review organizational charts, find who is who in your organization. You must know the key people in the organization who you are going to interact with.

- **Lines of Business** – Find if there are multiple lines of business and their share in overall business revenue and profit.

- **Products and Services** – Get to know Products and Services offered by your organization and their respective revenue. Find any future products and services that are in the pipeline.

- **Major Business Partners** – Find who are major business partners?

- **Budget Cycle** – When budget process starts and how projects are approved?

- **Important Customers** – Who are the largest customers?

- **Role of Technology** – How important role technology plays in the business? What major technologies are in currently being used?

- **Geography** – Is your organization engaged in international business? How many people it employs and where?

- **Major Competitors** – Find who are major competitors of your organization.

- **Stock Information** – If you are part of a publically traded company, find its stock and quarterly reports. How your stock has been fluctuating in past 12 months and why.

Following is a sample mind map. You can draw your own or expand on it. This will create a picture of the business in your mind and make it easy for you understand corporate dynamics.

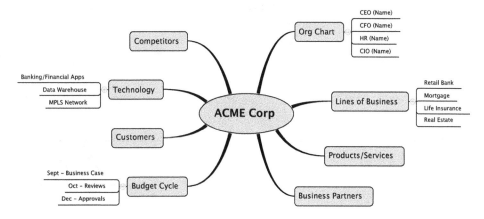

GOALS AND ACTIVITY LOG

Plan and record your activities related to the previous topic. I would suggest take one area of your mind map each week and write important people, processes, or technologies related to that area.

Date	Goal/Activity Description

4 The Business Lingo

The role of security professionals has evolved over time. You know the information security technology, however, you are going to get involved in "business" discussion quite often. Understanding and *speaking* business language is critical for your success as information security professional. It is also crucial for effective communication inside your organization.

If anyone of the following terms seem cryptic to you, there is a good likelihood that you need to learn some business terminology.

- **Accounting and Finance** – Present/Future Values, Amortizations, CAPEX and OPEX, Depreciation, Cash Flow, Net Present Value (NPV), Payback Period.

- **Marketing** – Impressions, CTR (Click Through Rate), Conversion Rate, Cost Per Thousand (CPT), Bounce Rate, Visits and Hits, Exposure, Infomercial, Search Engine Optimization (SEO).

- **Business Management** – Assets, Capital, B2B, Balance Sheet, Benchmarking, BPO, CGS, Supply Chain, Deming Cycle, Fiscal Year, Fixed and Variable Costs, GAAP, KPI, ROI, SWOT Analysis, Benchmarking.

- **Stock Market** – Market Capitalization, Quarterly/Annual Reports (8-K, 10-K, 10-Q), Dividend, public records, Options, Futures, Face Value, SEC, NYSE, Emerging Markets, Ratings, Basis Point, Book, Hedge, Index, Insider Trading, Venture Capital, Ticker.

- **Legal** – Trademarks and Service marks, copyrights, patents, deposition

In addition to the above, there are terms specific to your industry. For example, insurance industry has its own terminology like "liability coverage" and "reinsurance" that you need to learn if you are in working in an insurance company. Same is true for manufacturing, banking, retail, government, and other industry sectors.

SUGGESTED ACTIONS

- **Online Courses** – Take a basic finance course at Coursera (coursera.org), Udacity (udacity.com), Edx (edx.org), or iTunesU to understand basic finance.

- **Read Book(s)** – If you have not read it yet, buy "The Personal MBA" by Josh Kaufman and read it. Make a list of books that you would like to read in next 12 months and add these to the "Goals/Activity Log".

- **Financial Web Sites** – Review public company information on Google Finance and Yahoo Finance web sites for an introduction to quarterly reports, key personnel, and other business information.

- **Internal Courses** – Your organization may have internal courses to understand their business. Take some of these courses.

You can use the following mind map to mark you progress. Pick one are at one time and mark it when complete.

As always, don't shy away from creating your own mind map!

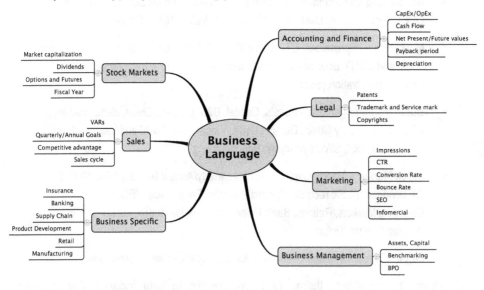

While learning the business language, make two sections of your learning goal: First, general business language and concepts and second, business language specific to your industry sector.

Goals and Activity Log

Plan and record your activities related to the previous topic.

Date	Goal/Activity Description

5 Aligning Corporate and Security Goals

Let us face it: In addition to strategy, everyone needs goals and objective to get things done and to measure progress/performance. In a typical organization, the CEO has a list of goals and objectives that trickle down through chain of leadership. Objective for IT leaders are usually derived from CEO objectives. Understanding the organizational objectives as well as the personalities of your CEO and CIO helps in creating and aligning the information security strategy.

Most of the business objectives fall into one of the following areas:

1. **Business goals** (e.g. increase revenue by X percent, open 20 new retail locations, mobile workforce)

2. **Industry drivers** (e.g. use of mobile apps, enable video, be compliant with a new standard)

3. **Internal issues and improvements** (e.g. improve response time of banking application)

Success of information security program is to manage risk while supporting the corporate goals and objectives. Understanding corporate objectives is the first step towards achieving this success.

SUGGESTED ACTIONS

- **Goal Alignment** – Find annual goals and objectives of your CEO and CIO. Make sure your strategy and projects are tied to one or more of these objectives.

- **Personality Understanding** – Understand CIO and CEO personalities, their approach towards IT and information security, do they like to build internal resources or rely more on vendors, etc. Take notes of important personality traits.

- **Periodic Review** – There may be a periodic review of corporate goals and objectives. Be part of this review and demonstrate how information security is helping in achieving corporate objectives. Risk management and information security budget management can be easily tied to organizational objectives. Schedule a quarterly review meeting for information security strategy.

- **Mutual Cooperation** – It is much easy to bundle security objectives with corporate goals. For example, if there is a planned redesign of an ecommerce application, you may be able to implement/enhance identity management as part of it.

You can use a mind map like the following to list corporate objectives and tie information security objectives with corporate objectives.

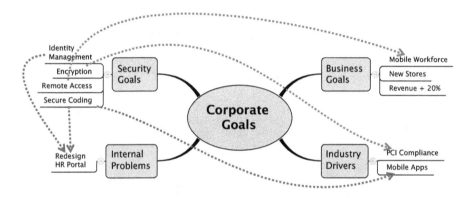

Remember it does not need to be a fancy mind map. Many times you can draw this type of maps on your white board simply by using dry erase markers.

GOALS AND ACTIVITY LOG

Plan and record your activities related to the previous topic.

Date	Goal/Activity Description

6 Budget Process and Funding Requests

Being creative during the budget process is critical for getting funding approval for projects with hard-to-show Return On Investment (ROI). By being creative, you can also use the budget process to promote information security causes and bundle security initiatives with other projects. Here are some ideas:

- **Partnerships** – Partner with other IT projects to bundle security in IT infrastructure projects, software development, even physical security.

- **Common Causes** – Create a win-win situation for you and your partners. It makes them look good as they show their "seriousness" about protecting company reputation while enabling business.

- **Split in Phases** – Splitting large initiative in multiple phases helps and builds credibility in your approach to solve problems. It shows you are thoughtful in visualizing the long-term goals.

- **Data Driven** – Plan well ahead of time for information security projects and gather data to support your projects at three levels (a) overall information security industry (b) related to your specific industry sector, and (c) related to your specific business. This data may be logs analysis, industry trends, and data breach reports.

SUGGESTED ACTIONS

Consider budget requests as an ongoing initiative throughout the year for building business cases and marketing your initiatives.

- **Follow Timing** – Many organizations have specific times of the year to propose new projects (may be a specific quarter of fiscal year). Understand the timing and plan ahead to have your project proposals ready.

- **Build Business Case** – Learn how to develop a formal business case. Go above and beyond the base requirements for building the business case.

- **Return on Investment** – Like other investments, the information security investments needs justification. Figure out how to calculate Return on Security Investment (ROSI) to justify the investment. Caution: it may not be easy!

- **Socialize** – Don't wait for the formal budget process to start. Start marketing your projects earlier to your leadership. Use one page strategy maps to elaborate your projects for easy marketing.

Use the following mind as a sample for each of your project budget requests. You can attach an expanded mind map with the budget request to show your due diligence.

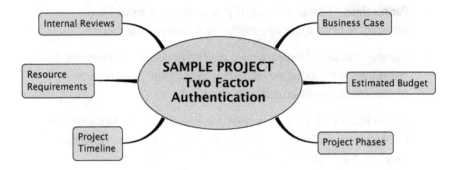

If you use a mind map like this in your budget requests, it shows that you have looked at different aspects of the project and has built a solid business case. Depending upon your organization's guideline, the process may be a little different. However, standardizing your budget requests to a well-thought-off template will help.

GOALS AND ACTIVITY LOG

Plan and record your activities related to the previous topic.

Date	Goal/Activity Description

7 Know Data, Insist for Data

Avoid fixing problems that don't exist. It is imperative that *decisions* (and opinions) are made based upon data and facts. There was a time in information security industry when data was not readily available. A number of reliable sources of data are available now and there is no reason to make decisions based upon market hype, aggressive vendor marketing, or personal likes/dislikes. Some of these data sources include research reports from security vendors, industry analysis, and online data gathering web sites. All of this can help you make informed decisions. Collecting and mining data from within your organization will also be of great value to you.

Some of the data sources are as follows and there are many more from reputable organizations.

- **Verizon DBIR** – Data Breach Investigation Report (DBIR) from Verizon is published on an annual basis and contains result of large number of data breach investigations.

- **Arbor DDoS Survey Report** – Arbor Networks publishes a comprehensive survey report about DDoS activity.

- **DatalossDB** – DatalossDB is an online source to record known data breaches (datalossdb.org).

- **Analyst Reports** – Gartner, Forrester and other industry analysts publish they analysis about information security on an ongoing basis.

- **Security Vendors** – Many security vendors including Imperva, Spider Labs/Trustwave, Cisco, Symantec, etc publish their own reports about information security that include useful data.

- **Internal Data Sources** – You have data coming from your internal systems including system logs, IDS/IPS alerts, Firewall permit/deny logs, successful/failed logins, Net flow data, FIM[1] and WAF[2] Logs.

Use these data sources for education and awareness in your monthly/quarterly leadership meetings as well as for building business cases for your projects.

SUGGESTED ACTIONS

1. **Subscriptions** – Subscribe to external data sources to make informed decisions and build business cases.

2. **Visualization Tools** – Use visualization tools and the security data for internal education and awareness purposes.

3. **Bust Wrong Assertions** – Insist on data to backup assertions made by information security team members as well by people outside information security. You can save tremendous amount of money and time by avoiding solutions and projects that have little to no value.

4. **Communicate** – Communicate data findings to the IT and business leadership. It will bring credibility to the information security team.

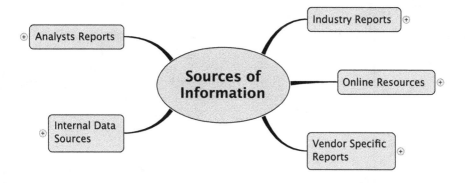

---

[1] FIM – File Integrity Monitoring tools used to detect unauthorized changes to file system.

[2] WAF – Web Application Firewall used for protecting web-based application and eCommerce.

GOALS AND ACTIVITY LOG

Plan and record your activities related to the previous topic.

Date	Goal/Activity Description

PART TWO

Information Security Strategy

8 Strategy Building Blocks

CISO is not an easy role to be in. The scope of CISO responsibilities spans almost all aspects of business in the form of risk management. This includes but not limited to security operations, compliance, architecture, business partners, legal, Human Resources, compliance, and overall risk management. The following diagram shows some of these areas. A high-resolution mind map of CISO responsibilities is available at the following URL:

http://rafeeqrehman.com/wp-content/uploads/2013/01/CISO_Job_Responsibilities_v3.pdf

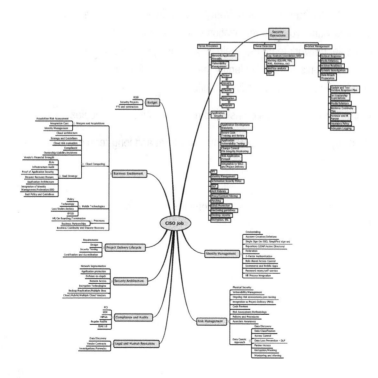

Managing everything with limited resources and a continuous battle of cost justification takes a lot of discipline. Prioritization, continuous risk assessment, establishing partnerships, and managing expectations are keys to a CISO success. Create an ongoing Plan-Do-Check-Act cycle and delegate as much as you can. Base your strategy on data, and create short-term tactical as well as long-term strategic goals.

This book is an effort to share the knowledge by learning from experiences of successful CISOs who are able to an order to this chaos.

SUGGESTED ACTIONS

- **Find Time to Strategize** – Don't get bogged by day-to-day work. Find some time to think about strategy.

- **Set Priorities** – Set priorities, as it would be difficult to focus on everything at the same time. You can set your priorities with a 3-year roadmap (or something similar).

- **Security is Shared Responsibility** – Security is everybody's responsibility. Find partners within your IT organization who can share some responsibilities. For example, network team may help in security operations. Server and desktop teams will have a stake in identity management. Partner with application development for secure coding practices.

- **Focus on Risk** – Focus on risk and not on specific technologies.

- **Strategy and Tactics** – Determine short-term and long-term goals that give best value for reducing risk.

- **Avoid Complexity** – Complexity is enemy of security. There is always a simpler way of doing things. If things look complex to people, most probably they are. Find ways to simplify them.

GOALS AND ACTIVITY LOG

Plan and record your activities related to the previous topic.

Date	Goal/Activity Description

9 Information Security SWOT Analysis

Understanding and analyzing the current situation when you walk into a new job or when establishing baseline is critical to your success. SWOT (Strengths, Weaknesses, Opportunities, Threats) is an industry standard way of analyzing the current situation and to make a basis for your strategy.

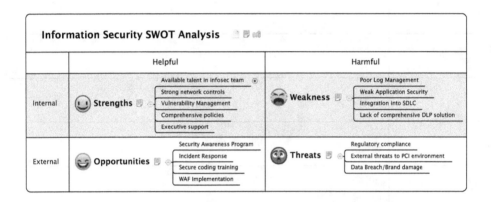

Following is a sample SWOT analysis for a security organization. You can use this as a template to create SWOT analysis of your own.

Note that opportunities may include items that can be implemented in short term and that may utilize existing investments in technology or processes.

You can use SWOT analysis to do the following:

- **New Job** – Starting a new job

- **Baseline** – Creating a baseline of current state of information security

- **Risk Assessment** – You can use SWOT analysis for periodic risk assessment

- **Strategy** – Creating or modifying information security strategy

- **Business Case** – To build business cases for budget process or request funding.

- **Marketing** – SWOT analysis diagram can be a good marketing tool for information security.

SUGGESTED ACTIONS

- **Use of Mind Mapping Tools** – SWOT analysis is one area where I would recommend using a mind mapping tool to enable you perform drill down exercises.

- **Interviews** – While doing SWOT analysis, do interviews within the information security team as well as other IT and business leaders.

- **Internal and External Factors** – List and analyze both internal and external factors that may impact SWOT analysis.

- **SWOT Analysis Uses** – Use results of SWOT analysis for improving strategy and as a basis for periodic risk assessment.

GOALS AND ACTIVITY LOG

Plan and record your activities related to the previous topic.

Date	Goal/Activity Description

10 What Are the Absolute Minimums?

Many information security leaders have a list of security controls and technologies they have implemented and still have to ask this question: Is this enough and what else can I do? Essentially, with a little more discussion, the question boils down to this: What are the base-minimum security controls and technologies that I need to implement?

While the answer varies depending upon a number of aspects including industry sector, threat agents, type and size of organization; there are four key security activities that every CISO and CIO should be looking at as listed below. Remember this is a step before you start looking at specific technologies or products.

1. **Risk Assessment** – Do periodic risk assessment and base all security
   product or process decisions on results of risk assessment.

2. **Threat Prevention** – The best way to deal with a threat is to prevent it from
   realizing. See the diagram below for some examples of threat prevention
   technologies.

3. **Threat Detection** – If a threat agent is able to penetrate your network, you
   should be able to detect it.

4. **Incident Response** – If you can't prevent or detect a threat, you should be
   prepared for responding to an incident as a last resort.

After making an assessment of current solutions in each of these areas, you can start looking at the technologies and actions you need to take as shown in diagram. I would highly recommend creating a diagram of your own and use it within the security team as well as for creating the awareness among IT leadership.

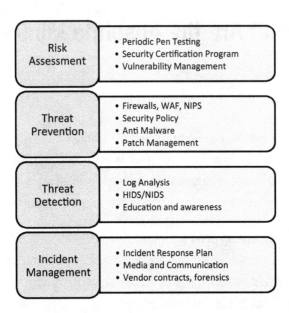

SUGGESTED ACTIONS

1. **Risk Assessment** – Periodic risk assessment has to be the basis of implementing information security solutions and controls. The threat landscape changes continuously and so should your strategy to mitigate the risk.

2. **Strong Policy** – A meaningful security policy is basis of any information security program. Ensure it is enforced and monitored properly and has full backing from the business leadership.

3. **Threat Prevention** – Ensure well-managed firewalls. In addition to inbound network traffic control, ensure outbound access is tightly controlled to put a barrier for data extrusion in case an attacker is able to get inside the network.

4. **Threat Detection** – Most of the data breaches are still detected by outside parties[3]. Ensure system have logging enabled and there is an active log monitoring. You should have a system to detect abnormalities in logs.

5. **Incident Response** – Perform a mock incident response just like a disaster recovery exercise. Get first responders trained on responding to incidents.

6. **Prepare for Incidents** – Have vendor contracts for forensic analysis in case of a data breach instead of building costly internal capability.

7. **Awareness Program** – Plan for a meaningful information security awareness program.

---

[3] Verizon data breach investigation report shows this trend year over year.

GOALS AND ACTIVITY LOG

Plan and record your activities related to the previous topic.

Date	Goal/Activity Description

11 Find Opportunities for Quick Results

Showing return on investment (ROI) in information security is difficult. Most of the time you are preventing bad things from happening. Proving absence of something is not an easy task and people can't easily visualize the results of an information security program.

As a leader and influencer, you need to show results not only to keep your team motivated but also to a broader audience in your organization. While focusing on a long-term strategy, you also need to find opportunities for tactical, smaller, and easy tasks that people can relate to and see the value of investments in information security.

- **Taking Small Steps** – Success is built on small steps that are taken in a direction. Create a strategy and identify parts of strategy that are quick and easy to implement.

- **Phased Approach** – If you can't find smaller steps, break big projects into smaller phases. Completing each phase will show progress.

- **Build Confidence** – Smaller goals and quick results build confidence and sense of achievement.

- **Small Step Do Matter** – Everything does not need to be earth shattering.

- **Take Feedback** – Taking feedback may reveal small issues related to information security that can be target of achieving quick results.

Remember, while big achievement matter in the long term, smaller things are the ones that build your rapport and trust inside your organization.

Suggested Actions

Following is list of some actions that can create immediate value.

- **Use SWOT** – Use "Opportunities" part of SWOT analysis to find quick hits.

- **Simplify Processes** – Simplify at least one process on a monthly basis. People will see immediate value in your leadership when you solve their problems.

- **Make Security Problem Solver** – Ask someone in your team to write a small script to count number of "deny" events in firewall logs. Other people outside the security team may use this to troubleshoot their problems. Go a step further to segregate the data for each firewall to show which firewalls are more/less effective.

- **Arrange Training** – Arrange training on some security topic for people who don't report to you. Keep it simple. An example will be how to secure your home network.

- **Arrange Vendor Briefings** – Ask a vendor/partner to come and brief IT organization on a technology on your roadmap. Invite your peers to the presentation. Once you get comfortable, you can even invite multiple vendors for an in-house security summit.

- **Short Term Risk Assessment** – Pick one or two systems every quarter and perform risk assessment on those.

There are many other things within your organization that are small and easy to do. Talk to your peers and they will give you ideas and tell their problems and things that are near and dear to them.

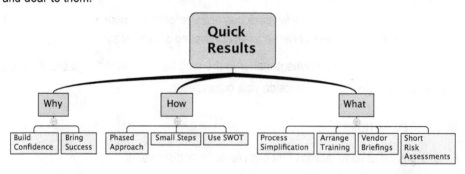

GOALS AND ACTIVITY LOG

Plan and record your activities related to the previous topic.

Date	Goal/Activity Description

12 Pitfalls of "MORE" Security Controls

More security controls "should" be better. Isn't it? Talking about "pitfalls of more security" seems to be counter-intuitive initially! However, you need people to implement and manage security controls *effectively*. The fact is that most of the organizations don't have enough people or recourses to effectively implement and manage even base level security controls. As a result, security products are purchased and are either not implemented or not managed properly, failing to realize return on investment (ROI). So before you buy a next cool product and embark on creating a new process or control, ask yourself the questions like the following:

- **Resource Management** – If you have more security products to manage than available resources, none of these will be managed properly that may actually put you at more risk by giving false sense of security.

- **Effective Use of Existing Technologies** – When was the last time the security team performed a firewall rule audit or an IPS policy review to ensure their effectiveness?

- **Monitoring** – How sure are you that someone in your team is actively monitoring and managing system and application logs? If that is not the case, it may be a good place to use your energy and resources. Verizon data breach investigation report (DBIR) shows the most of the data breaches have the information in log files and an effective log review could have avoided data breaches.

- **Identity Management** – In the past six months, has anyone looked at user or application accounts/IDs to identify default/weak passwords or IDs that are no longer in use. Do you know which accounts have more access than they need to?

- **Data Location** – Have you done a catalog of all data stores inside the company? Data is the asset you are trying to protect. How sure are you about where this asset resides?

- **Risk Assessment** – Do you do a meaningful risk assessment of your organization every six months or at least every year?

If answers to any of these questions is not making you feel good, it is better to take initiative to implement solutions around these tasks before you worry too much about the next media hype. Most of the data breaches involve criminals who want to steel and sell your customer or employee data and make money. They are after easy targets. Basic security is what you need before you implement any super sophisticated and expensive solution with lofty (and often false) promises.

Remember that implementing additional technologies will take the focus away from these basics tasks and evidence shows that attacker behind most of the data breaches don't really employ sophisticated techniques. Most of the attacks are preventable by employing baseline security controls. Keep your focus on basics. More controls can be bad as you will end up doing too many things and none will be effective. *Take new initiatives only when you have covered the basics.*

SUGGESTED ACTIONS

Keep your focus on basic security controls. The data from different reports show that covering basics brings a great value to an information security program.

- **Log Reviews** – Identify log sources, including application logs, and implement a process to review logs.

- **Make Best Use of Existing Technologies** – If you have firewalls, IPS/IDS, FIM, or other technologies, make best use of these by policy tuning, alerting, and logging.

- **Catalog Information Assets** – Identify locations of all critical data and enable simple controls like logging and FIM on these critical assets.

- **Access Controls** – It is very likely you already have a technology in your company to implement access controls and monitor unauthorized access. Just start using it.

- **Risk Based Decisions** – As mentioned in other parts of this book, base all your decisions on risk and data instead of industry hype. The risk assessment must drive decisions to implement new controls or security solutions.

GOALS AND ACTIVITY LOG

Plan and record your activities related to the previous topic.

Date	Goal/Activity Description

13 Information Security Strategy Drivers

There are three main drivers for any information security strategy or program. Understanding these drivers is key to creating an effective information security strategy. These drivers are as follows:

1. Risk Management

2. Compliance Needs

3. Business Goals and Objectives

These three drivers should dictate information security operations including threat detection, mitigation, and response.

- **Risk Management** – The risk management requires periodic risk assessment including changes in threat landscape, results of pen testing, organizational and industry specific risk assessment work, change in technologies or evolution of new technologies, etc.

- **Compliance** – Compliance needs are usually mandatory and may include compliance to government laws, regulations, or industry standards. Examples are privacy laws, Sarbanes-Oxley act, PCI, different privacy laws in different regions/countries, and many others.

- **Business Goals** – Business goals and objectives may include moving to cloud computing, cost management, outsourcing/insourcing, expansion to other countries, mergers and acquisitions and any other goals set by business and technology leadership. All of these need involvement of information security.

Each elements of information security strategy must map to one or more items in these categories. Highest priority items can be determined by finding overlap of all three drivers. Next level of priority will include strategy elements that cover two of the three drivers. Please refer to the attached diagram showing overlap of these drivers.

ACTION ITEMS

The following action items help a CISO and other leaders in information security to formulate a better security strategy.

1. **Utilize Results of Previous Risk Assessments** – Create a list of all open items from previous risk assessments as an input to information security strategy.

2. **Identify Business Drivers** – Create a list of all business drivers. You may get help from corporate strategy to find CEO and CIO business objectives.

3. **Identify Compliance Needs** – Create a list of all compliance needs, the laws, and industry standards your organization has to comply with.

4. Build a mapping of your security strategy elements to risk items, business drivers and compliance needs. Every element in the information security strategy must map to one of the drivers. If, for any reason, you are not able to map a driver to one of the three areas, create a new category but try to avoid too many categories.

5. **Find Overlaps** – Finds area of overlap and set priorities for information security strategy elements.

6. **Get Feedback** – Share this mapping with your team and peers and get their feedback to validate your findings.

GOALS AND ACTIVITY LOG

Plan and record your activities related to the previous topic.

Date	Goal/Activity Description

14 Make Cloud Part of Your Information Security Strategy

While CISOs across the globe are being asked to be provide guidelines for moving business applications to cloud computing platforms, the trend of moving security services to cloud is also picking up steam. Partly because CISOs have to protect business applications in the cloud (hence the need for cloud based security solutions) and partly because some security services just makes sense to be in the cloud. Following are some information security services that you can include in your cloud security services strategy.

- **DDoS Defence** – Protection against Distributed Denial of Service (DDoS) attacks using cloud based solutions makes perfect sense. Most of times it is already too late to put any counter measures at your premises when you are under DDoS attack. It is very likely that your Internet services providers have a DDoS defense service that you can benefit from.

- **Email and Web Content Filtering** – Rather than implementing an in-house solution for email and web filtering, cloud-based services make more sense both from a cost and administration perspectives. Many organizations already use cloud services in web and email content filtering.

- **Firewalls and IPS** – Many Internet services provides now offer cloud based firewalls and IPS solutions. These solutions can save money. You don't need hardware, software licensing, and fulltime employees to manage these devices for updates and patches.

- **DLP** – Cloud based Data Loss Prevention (DLP) solution in conjunction with email and web content filtering can be very effective.

- **IDM** – IDentity Management (IDM), especially for ecommerce, retail, and healthcare industries provide quick implementation and easy administration.

Two-factor authentication and federation are much easy to implement using cloud technologies.

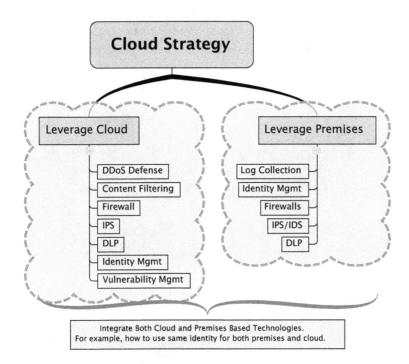

- **Vulnerability Management** – Cloud based vulnerability management systems are already quite popular. These include both network and application vulnerability scanning solutions and are available from multiple vendors.

- **PKI** - A cloud based Public Key Infrastructure can save significant cost and improve risk posture.

ACTION ITEMS

1. **Financial Analysis** – Do a cost-benefit analysis to compare cloud based security services with in-house implementation over 3-5 years of time. Include hardware, licensing, support, training, and FTE (full time employee) costs into the equation.

2. **Blended Approach** – To take advantages of cloud based security services, review your current strategy and identify cloud based services that blend into your strategy.

3. **Integrate Premises and Cloud Technologies** – Ensure these services integrate into a centralized monitoring and management scheme.

4. **Create Cloud Strategy** – Make sure new services are cloud-ready and work for on-premises and in-cloud IT infrastructure. Even if you are not currently hosting any business applications in cloud, you may get there soon.

GOALS AND ACTIVITY LOG

Plan and record your activities related to the previous topic.

Date	Goal/Activity Description

15 Single Page Strategy

In other parts of this book, you have seen CISO responsibility mind maps with large number of items. This could be very intimidating for many people and confusing too. Many of these items are related to day-to-day operations. An essential part of strategy is that it must be shared among non-security IT and business leaders. It is imperative that the strategy must be simple and easy to understand for executives.

When talking about strategy, the effective way is to make it look simple by taking complexities out.

- **Visually Appealing** – Your audience should be able to easily able to see the strategy in the form of a high-level block diagram.

- **Make it Simple** – It should be simple enough such that the audience can understand it.

- **Summarize** – Although the strategy detailed document may be long, the visual presentation should be on a single page.

- **Related** – The strategy has to be related to business objectives.

Following is a short version of single page strategy. Use the expanded version for longer presentation only. For regular conversations, only use the top five points.

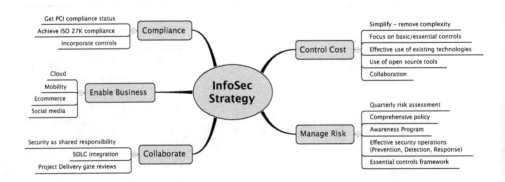

ACTION ITEMS

1. **PowerPoint Slid or Mind Map** – Condense your strategy into a single-page PowerPoint slide or a mind map. Visual presentation showing relationship of different components is very critical for this.

2. **Share** – Make sure the information security team, your peers, and any other stake holder has a copy of this page.

3. **Communicate** – Keep the strategy page with you in all meetings and find opportunities to explain it over and over at different occasions. It takes time for people to understand things and repetition is a key.

4. **Simplify** – Over time, you will figure out the areas of the strategy diagram that are difficult for people to grasp. Simplify the document based upon feedback from others.

I worked in a company where the CEO used the same single-page power point diagram for three years to explain his strategy in all hands meetings. With this repetition, almost everybody in the company knew major points of the corporate strategy.

GOALS AND ACTIVITY LOG

Plan and record your activities related to the previous topic.

Date	Goal/Activity Description

16 Be Champion of New Technologies

Ready or not, new technologies will come along. The latest additions are mobile devices and cloud computing. It has been web services and AJAX in the recent past. Big Data, Hadoop, and distributed analytics are coming soon if you are not already there. Remember that if there is a business need, your organization will adopt new technologies no matter what. Better be ready instead of playing a catch up game.

- **Adopt or Be Irrelevant** – There are only two choices: resist the adoption and put yourself into the risk of becoming irrelevant or be proactive and champion adoption of new technologies.

- **Help in Competitive Advantage** – New technologies are business enablers and provide competitive advantage. Be an agent in creating competitive advantage for your business.

- **Be Early Adopter** – Being a leader, you have to help your organization become early adopter. Security leaders in other organizations will look toward you as an early adapter and you will establish your leadership.

- **Help Change Perception** – By championing new technologies, you can change perception of information security as a business enabler instead of "killer of innovation".

- **Retain Talent** – You can better engage members of your information security team by assigning them research on new technologies. It is a win-win situation for every person involved as well as for your organization to retain talent.

SUGGESTED ACTIONS

You can take the following actions in helping you and your team engaged in adoption of new technologies.

1. **Identify Relevant Emerging Technologies** – Perform a quick business analysis to identify emerging technologies that are related to business of your organization.

2. **Engage Information Security Team** – Assign each of the identified technologies to research-minded members of information security team.

3. **Arrange Vendor Information Session** – Vendors of emerging technologies are hungry to find organizations who are willing to listen to them. Invite reputable vendors and business leaders in your organization to understand how you can benefit from these technologies.

4. **Target the Message** – For your internal audience, create an effective message showing you are keen to be proactive so that new technologies can be adopted in a secure manner and manage the risk.

GOALS AND ACTIVITY LOG

Plan and record your activities related to the previous topic.

Date	Goal/Activity Description

17 Embrace Mobility and Cloud

Cloud computing and mobile devices are here to stay. Industry is moving fast towards adoption of both mobility and cloud. You have to deal with personal mobile devices, cloud based storage, cloud based disaster recovery solutions, and many other initiatives. Without cloud and mobility, it will be difficult for any organization to do business, just like email is critical for business although initially many people thought it would create security and data leakage problems.

- **Current Use of Cloud** – Is your organization using Cloud based services currently? Most probably it is. Many organizations are already using cloud based solutions like Salesforce, HR, Applicant Tracking Systems, Payroll, etc.

- **Managing Risk** – Are there new risk scenarios to take care of? Absolutely. However, the risk is manageable and in some cases the risk may be actually lower for cloud technologies than premises based solutions. There is nothing totally risk free. The key is to manage the risk instead of running away from it.

- **Hype** – Don't pay attention to hype of "more" risk in cloud computing. You have to do due diligence and many organizations are able to manage risk very effectively.

- **Competitive Advantage** – Use of cloud computing and mobility as another competitive advantage to your organization. In many cases your organization can take advantage of converting capital expense to operational expense. Cloud computing is also great in providing better agility.

SUGGESTED ACTIONS

- **Create Strategy** – As a first step, create strategy for mobile devices, personal mobile devices, and cloud computing.

- **Create Policy** – Back the corporate strategy with policy and procedures.

- **Identify Compliance Needs** – Identify all compliance needs and ensure these are part of strategy and policy. In some cases laws may require data to be stored within certain geographic boundaries.

- **Identify Specific Solutions** – Cloud computing is not one product or service. There are many aspects of cloud that could be advantageous to your organization. Some of the solutions include cloud storage, disaster recovery, compute resources, multi-tenant infrastructure and applications. Identify specific solutions for your organization and be proactive in creating policies around those.

- **Different Paradigm** – Cloud computing and mobile devices have shifted traditional paradigm of business applications. Create procedures and controls for things like cloud-enabled software development, encryption, data communications, etc. Many of the security controls that are great for traditional data center may not work for cloud environment.

- **Cloud Security Certification** – Get some people on information security certified for cloud security. One such certification is CCSK.

GOALS AND ACTIVITY LOG

Plan and record your activities related to the previous topic.

Date	Goal/Activity Description

18 Security Considerations for Purchasing SaaS Solutions

More and more organizations are buying Software as a Service (SaaS) solutions. These solutions include but not limited to human resource management, payroll, job posting and applicant tracking, sales management, Customer Relationship Management (CRM), and others. This trend is expected to continue and even accelerate over coming years as cloud adoption increases. There are number of benefits to this trend including smaller cost of ownership, moving CAPEX[4] to OPEX[5], transferring upgrades and patch management to a third party, and keeping focus on core business, among others.

Decisions for purchasing SaaS applications should include factors like the following. Asking these questions and collecting information will help make better decisions.

- **Vendor Financial Strength** – Determine financial stability of the SaaS vendor, years of operations, and existing customer references.

- **Proof of Application Security** – Demand software application security testing report. All SaaS vendors must have periodic testing of their applications or certification from a third party.

- **IT Infrastructure Audits** – Ask for independent audit report. Absence of independent audit may indicate lack of processes on the vendor side.

- **SLA** – Review Service Level Agreements (SLA) including penalties for not meeting SLA.

---

[4] Capital Expense

[5] Operational Expense

- **Disaster Recovery Planning** – Make sure you have a high level description of Disaster Recovery (DR) plans from the SaaS vendor.

- **Application Architecture** – Ask for high-level application architecture diagrams.

- **Identity Management** – Verify that the SaaS application integrates into your internal identity management system, federation, SSO, role based access.

SUGGESTED ACTIONS

In many cases some business unit will purchase a SaaS application *without* due diligence and without consulting information security team. To avoid this type of situation, implement the following controls.

- **SaaS Policy** – Proactively create a policy document that requires security testing and audit reports of the SaaS applications.

- **Purchasing Guidelines** – Provide a guideline document to internal audience to help them choose a SaaS vendor. These guidelines should include all factors mentioned above.

- **Vendor Research** – Do a due diligence for any previous incidents on the SaaS vendor side using public resources.

The following mind map will help in summarizing and creating awareness for SaaS strategy.

GOALS AND ACTIVITY LOG

Plan and record your activities related to the previous topic.

Date	Goal/Activity Description

19 Indicators of Successful Strategy

How do you know you have a sound information security strategy and reliable information security operations? Although the answer is not quite easy, there are some indicators that can point to it. First of all, do you think your security organization can operate without you or any other key person? If the answer is no, it is a red flag and you need to work on your security program to make it less dependent on specific people.

Following are some other important indicators of a successful or flawed strategy.

1. **Mature Processes** – Can you have a vacation without the fear of someone going wrong? If the answer is negative, it typically shows lack of sound processes and procedures.

2. **Great Awareness Program** – Do people reach out to you with questions related to information security? If the answer is yes, you are doing something good with security awareness program.

3. **SDLC Integration** – Is information security team notified during initiation of a new project, testing, and implementation? If yes, you are engaged in cross-team processes and in the project delivery lifecycle.

4. **Leadership** – Is information security part of agenda for quarterly and annual meetings? If not, you need to work on "selling" security to leadership.

5. **Team** – Are members of information security team generally happy and not overwhelmed. Do they understand the strategy and that every battle is not worth fighting?

This is not a comprehensive list of everything you should be looking for. The point I would like to make is you should always be evaluating success and effectiveness of information security program. There is always room for improvement.

SUGGESTED ACTIONS

- **Most Important Audience of Strategy** – First and the most important audience of your strategy is the information security team. Collaborate with the team in creation and implementation of strategy.

- **Communicate** – Make sure all members of information security team understand the strategy and know the future plans. Communicating the strategy is always better than keeping it secret.

- **Metrics Review** – Create a metrics about effectiveness[6] of your strategy and review it on quarterly basis. For example, new vulnerabilities discovered by your vulnerability scanner should have a downward trend over time.

- **Improvement List** – Create a list of indicators that need improvement and set deadlines and actions to improve these indicators.

- **Security Feeling** – A lot of security is about "feeling[7]". Think about things that you can do to improve feeling about information security. Every organization and its culture is different and your approach about improving the feeling may be different tool.

---

[6] Matrix like Key Performance Indicators (KPI).

[7] Bruce Schneier – The Psychology of Security - http://www.schneier.com/essay-155.html

GOALS AND ACTIVITY LOG

Plan and record your activities related to the previous topic.

Date	Goal/Activity Description

20 Compliance is Result of Good Security

Compliance is a part of information risk management and each security program has to deal with compliance needs. However, basing information security strategy solely on compliance needs is not a great idea. Organizations may be compliant with laws and industry regulations and may still have high risk in some areas.

The main point to remember is that compliance is a result of a good information security program, not vice versa. All compliance requirements (and security frameworks) are looking for specific information security controls that must be part of information security program in the first place.

- **Cause and Effect** – Good information security practice will result in compliance irrespective of your compliance needs. Focus on good information security controls rather than some checkboxes.

- **Organizational Needs are Different** – Depending upon your organization type and business, information security needs may be different. You may need controls that are not covered by compliance requirements or to protect against emerging threats.

- **Education and Awareness** – Many business executives are more concerned about compliance than security. A continuous effort is needed to reverse the order.

SUGGESTED ACTIONS

- **Understand Compliance Standards** – Create a list of all compliance standards that your organization needs to comply with.

- **Map Compliance Requirements to Controls** – Map compliance to list of security controls to ensure all items are covered.

- **Apply Risk Based Approach** – Don't try to fill check boxes. Apply a risk based approach to compliance. If a control can't be met, there may be mitigating or compensating controls.

- **Focus on Big Picture** – Focus on overall information security strategy and big picture. Also make sure that your auditors look at the bigger picture.

- **Apply Data Driven Approach** – While making risk decisions towards compliance, backup your decisions by data.

GOALS AND ACTIVITY LOG

Plan and record your activities related to the previous topic.

Date	Goal/Activity Description

21 Get Help to Build Business Cases

Excluding the organizations that have information security as their primary business, security is more or less a cost center[8]. Building a business case to implement information security programs always needs some creative thinking. The good news is that you don't have to build the business cases alone! Many security vendors have helpful advice, information, and case studies to build business cases. The best thing is that most of this information and consultation from security vendors is totally free to you, and you should take advantage of this information. Trusted external parties (like trusted vendors) bring credibility to discussions and sometimes help settle internal political issues as well.

Other platforms for getting help may be local CISO forum consisting of information security leaders like you, local ISSA chapters, or other non-vendor organizations. You should join such a forum and benefit from the ideas that other security leaders share in these forums. If there is no such forum in your city, start one.

Some of the ways you can use these free resources to your advantage are as follows:

- **Executive Security Briefing** – Bring consultants from your trusted security vendor/partner for an executive information security briefing in your organization.

- **Data Breach Investigation Report Briefing** – Verizon Data Breach Investigation Report (DBIR) is a de facto industry standard. Invite your executive team for a presentation on Verizon data breach investigation report. In a number of cases you board members or CEO may give you a go ahead for your projects as they get to know how data breaches are happening and understand the risk better.

---

[8] There is noting wrong with being cost center. There are many other cost centers like legal.

- **Provide Context** – In such briefings, provide context to your business leaders about how the discussion and findings relates to your organization.

- **Use Data to Build Business Case** – Use "real data" to build business cases. Industry reports, case studies, white papers, Verizon Data Breach Investigation Report, and analyst (Gartner, Forrester, etc) provide significant amount of data to build your business case.

SUGGESTED ACTION ITEMS

- **Build Vendor Relations** – Identify your trusted security vendors and engage them in your strategic initiatives. Make trusted vendors part of your strategy.

- **Plan Calendar Events** – Have at least one data breach investigation report briefing for your business leadership annually. Plan it ahead of time.

- **Join Local CISO Forum** – Join local CISO forum (or start one).

GOALS AND ACTIVITY LOG

Plan and record your activities related to the previous topic.

Date	Goal/Activity Description

22 Make Sure People Feel Valued

Everybody needs to have a sense of purpose and meaning in work. People give you the best of their dedication and their productivity when they feel like they are doing something that matters. Make sure you make them feel that way, not only information security team but others as well. People will do their best and go above and beyond to accomplish things when they are valued.

- **Give More Credit** – Always give people around you extra credit and recognition for their work.

- **Success is Team Work** - Try to use "I" as few times as you can. Success is a teamwork and it should be recognized as such. It is not easy, though.

- **Make Other Look Good** – Make your people look good in public, meetings, and among your peers and they will make you look good.

- **Earn Trust** – Trust is always earned and one way to ear the trust is leading by example.

There are many articles available on the Internet on this subject. The main point is to understand the importance as a strategy, find your shortcomings, and continuously working to make improvements.

SUGGESTED ACTIONS

- **Understand Talent** – Understand strengths of your team. Have individual lunch meetings with each team members and try not to talk about technology and focus on understanding their personalities as a whole.

- **Understand Personal Interests** – Make a list of items that interest your direct reports, including their hobbies.

- **Provide Tools** – Buy each of them at least one security tool of their interest.

- **Hackathon Day** – Designate one day of the month as a "hackathon day" and let people do something out of normal routine.

- **Challenge** – Ask each member of your team to come up with a "side project" they would like to do and help them accomplish this project.

- **Focus on Achievements** – Focus and recognize achievements of each member, frequently!

GOALS AND ACTIVITY LOG

Plan and record your activities related to the previous topic.

Date	Goal/Activity Description

Part Three

Security Operations

23 Big Picture of Security Operations

Many InfoSec leaders spend majority of their time in information security operations and it does not have to be that way. Effective information security operations are about picking the basic essentials and *doing them right*. Running too many "*average*" security solutions may actually damage security posture compared to being excellent in basics.

- **Create List** – Mapping out all security operations requirements gives you an idea about everything you need to take care of on day-to-day basis. Following are two sample diagrams for mapping. You can create your own.

- **Policy and Procedures** – Start with policy documents for each area of security operations and then create procedures.

- **Delegate** – The security team does not and should not be responsible for all security operations. Determine other teams who can take ownership of some security operations and delegate. Ensure policy and procedures exists before delegation.

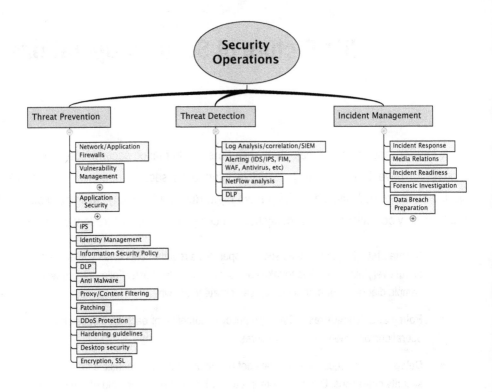

SUGGESTED ACTIONS

I suggest going through the following step for effective information security operations.

- **Create Mind Map** – I would highly suggest creating a mind map for your operational needs similar to the one shown above.

- **Own, Delegate, Defer** – From the mind map, take ownership of essentials, delegate anything that other teams can manage and defer non-essentials until you have resources to do them well. Focus on building business case to get resources for deferred items.

In the following section of the book, you will go through some of the important operational aspects but not everything required. The focus of this book is *not* an operational manual but to keep focus on strategy and the big picture.

GOALS AND ACTIVITY LOG

Plan and record your activities related to the previous topic.

Date	Goal/Activity Description

24 Major Operational Programs

Without going into detail, this chapter is to provide a list of programs necessary for the baseline security operations. Depending upon risk analysis, you may shorten or lengthen the list and also go into detail of each part.

1. **Log Monitoring** – Effective log monitoring is the most important operational program that any organization can have. Log monitoring has to be a building block of threat detection strategy. It can't be emphasized enough.

2. **Vulnerability Management** – Every organization needs a comprehensive vulnerability management program that includes network, applications, and physical vulnerabilities.

3. **Data Loss Prevention (DLP)** – Data loss prevention (DLP) is not name of a product but a comprehensive strategy that include network, desktops, mobile devices, paper, and other forms of data. It starts with data discovery and data classification before you think about implementing any technology.

4. **Intrusion Detection and Preventions** – This program should include network and host based intrusion detection, prevention, and alerting including monitoring of unauthorized changes aka file integrity monitoring.

5. **Security Certification** – The security certification program is part of project delivery and software development lifecycles to create a culture of implementing new products and services in a secure way.

6. **Incident and Data Breach Response** – Preparation for responding to information security incidents will make a huge difference for managing risk.

7. **Identity Management Program** – The identity management is becoming more critical with evidence of the use of stolen/weak credentials being used in data breaches. Include single sign on, federations, strong password controls coupled with multi factor authentication, and revocation of unused identities as part of this program. You can't manage access control without a strong identity management program.

Some of these programs are discussed in a little detail in the following sections. The objective is not to recommend any products or vendors but to emphasize on components of a successful security operations program.

SUGGESTED ACTIONS

- **Risk Assessment** – A risk assessment is necessary to find gaps and important items in information security operation. Create a time line to do risk assessment twice a year.

- **Prioritize** – Based upon risk assessment, prioritize which programs need your attention and make them part of information security roadmap.

GOALS AND ACTIVITY LOG

Plan and record your activities related to the previous topic.

Date	Goal/Activity Description

25 Log Monitoring and Management

Log management is difficult, time consuming, needs resources but is very important operational task. Many organizations struggle to implement an effective log monitoring and management solution.

- **Comprehensive Solution** – A comprehensive log monitoring solution must include both private data centers as well as cloud environment.

- **Assume Breach** – While creating a log management and monitoring solution, assume a breach has already happened and you are working on identifying it.

- **No Selective Logging** – Collecting all *appropriate* logs is essential. Selecting logging may result in missing important clues.

- **Log Correlation** – Correlation solutions are not easy to implement. Getting outside expertise may be needed to implement correlation. You can use an in-house SIEM solution or rely on a managed security services provider.

- **Netflow Data** – Collecting Netflow data can help in determining anomalies.

- **Implementing IP black/white lists** at network level can help. Many vendors provide options to include monitoring for watch lists.

SUGGESTED ACTIONS

- **Create Logging Scope** – Understand and create scope consisting of all devices that need to have logging enabled. In addition to system logs, include applications, antivirus, FIM, firewalls, IDS/IPS, and network devices in the scope of logging.

- **Right Type of Logging** – Ensure all devices under scope log "right type" of events. In many cases, important events may not be logged. Or even worst, unimportant events may be logged creating noise.

- **Centralized Logging And Analysis** – Create a system for centralized logging and analysis. Log correlation is important.

- **Determine Anomalies** – It is important to pay special attention to anomalies including but not limited to:

    o Sudden increases or decrease in logs.

    o Sudden increase in successful logins for regular user accounts.

    o New sources of login attempts based upon geo IP data.

    o Missing logs from certain servers or other hosts.

- **Alerting on Critical Events** – Enable alerting on critical events and make it part of security metrics.

- **Automated Reports** – Daily automated reports do help to determine anomalies.

GOALS AND ACTIVITY LOG

Plan and record your activities related to the previous topic.

Date	Goal/Activity Description

26 Vulnerability Management

Vulnerability management is a multitude of tasks including but not limited to vulnerability scanning, patch management, code review, pen testing, etc. It is a cyclical and ongoing process consisting of identifying, classifying, and mitigating of vulnerabilities. Vulnerability management is a fundamental information security control that every organization must have and make it part of the information security strategy.

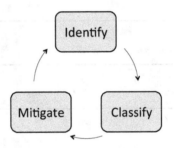

- **Not A Single Solution** – Vulnerability management is not a single solution or a scanning practice. It includes multiple aspects of a comprehensive program as mentioned above.

- **Consistency** – Consistency in vulnerability management is critical. It is a repeated and ongoing process.

- **Comprehensiveness** – Include all production and non-production system in vulnerability management program. Vulnerability in a "less important" system may result in data breach or may be used as a launching pad to attack other systems.

- **Risk Based Approach** – Vulnerability management can be very time consuming. Classifying vulnerabilities is a must so that high-risk vulnerabilities can be prioritized. Without a risk assessment process, vulnerability classification will not be very useful.

SUGGESTED ACTION ITEMS

1. **Create Scope** – It is critical to create scope of vulnerability management and treat it as a program. Include operating systems, databases, network equipment, and applications in the program.

2. **Selecting Scanning Service** – Most of the well-known vulnerability scanning services are comparable and similar in features and value. Select a service that provides API for integration into other systems.

3. **All Hosts Are Important** – Ensure all hosts, network and security devices, are part of the scope of vulnerability scanning.

4. **Standard Builds** – Create standard hardened builds for all operating systems, middleware, and databases.

5. **Comprehensive and Risk Based Patching** – Make sure *every* host is patched, even if patch implementation is not very aggressive. Do risk analysis for frequency of patching.

6. **Application Vulnerabilities are Important** – Give application level vulnerabilities the highest priority. Most of the data breaches exploit application flaws.

7. **Verify Fixes** – Make sure vulnerabilities are documented and tracked and fixes are verified.

8. **Measure Progress** – Create a baseline and measure progress. Use awareness program

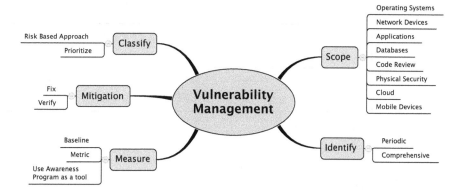

GOALS AND ACTIVITY LOG

Plan and record your activities related to the previous topic.

Date	Goal/Activity Description

27 Application Security and SDLC

Latest research reports (e.g. Verizon DBIR, Imperva) show that more and more attacks are directed towards applications and this trend is increasing due to multiple reasons, including the following:

- **Direct Access to Data** – Most attacks on information technology systems are financially motivated. Applications provide easy and in some cases direct access to data, which is valuable to attackers.

- **Open Access** – Firewalls don't block access to applications, which means attackers don't need to go through/exploit network security controls.

- **Lack of Maturity** – Most of the organization are doing better job on network and operating system security but application security is still lagging behind.

Fixing application security defects in production is more difficult, takes more time, and is quite costly. As a CISO or as a person in the position of ensuring security of the applications, you are better off making architecture review and application vulnerability testing as part of the Software Development Life Cycle (SDLC) or as part of project delivery process.

There are a number of commercial SaaS tools available for application security testing. Open source and free tools are also available for application testing.

SUGGESTED ACTION ITEMS

Some of the following actions cost very little and go a long way in implementing application security.

- **Create Standards for Application Development** – Create corporate standards for application development that should be based upon established research like the:

- o OWASP top ten web application security risks - https://www.owasp.org/index.php/Top_10

- o Safecode - http://www.safecode.org/publications/SAFECode_Dev_Practices0211.pdf

- o Recommendations from Verizon data breach investigation report - http://www.verizonbusiness.com/Products/security/dbir/

- o BISMM – Building Security in Maturity Model (BISMM) is a good resource for security in software. You can visit web site http://bsimm.com/facts for more information and a copy of framework.

- o WASC – Web applications security consortium threat classification at http://projects.webappsec.org/f/WASC-TC-v2_0.pdf

- **Secure Code Training** – Make ongoing training for software developers as part of security awareness program.

- **Security Testing** – Application testing has to be part of SDLC to ensure high-risk security vulnerabilities are fixed before moving code to production.

- **Change Management and Monitoring** – Implement a tight control over unauthorized application changes. This control must go beyond regular change control process and must able to detect changes to application software (e.g. file integrity monitoring).

- **WAF Implementation** – Proper implementation of a Web Application Firewall (WAF) provides good return on security investment. Make this part of your application security strategy.

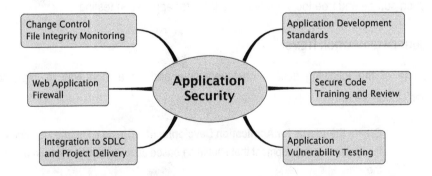

GOALS AND ACTIVITY LOG

Plan and record your activities related to the previous topic.

Date	Goal/Activity Description

28 Be Ready To Handle a Data Breach!

Many security professionals and CISOs are worried about being in a position of handling a data breach. You are not alone. Turn your fear into strength by taking steps mentioned below.

The biggest favor you can do to your organization (and yourself) is to be ready for a data breach. Some organizations emerge stronger out of a massive data breach while others have gone bankrupt. The difference is how prepared you are to handles a data breach.

Ask the following questions to your staff and yourself. If a satisfactory answer does not exist, it indicates a gap in your preparedness and planning to handle data breaches. Create action items to close the gaps.

- **Updated Incident Response (IR) Plan** – Do we have an incident response plan? When it was last updated?

- **IR Plan Testing** – Has the plan been tested using a mock incident just like testing disaster recovery plans?

- **Media Relations** – Who is the media coordinator to inform your customers about data breach? Is there is a sample communication letter ready and reviewed by legal department?

- **Reasonable Leadership Expectations** – Do your CIO and CEO recognize that even with all security controls and investment, there is still a reasonable probability of happening a data breach? Don't scare them but set reasonable expectations.

- **Integration to Business Continuity Planning** – What are the alternates if a critical business application or system is not available as a result of data breach or security incident?

- **Forensic Partner** – Do you have a vendor contract to help you in incident response and investigation if a data breach happens?

- **Insurance Policy** – Has your company purchased an insurance policy to cover a possible data breach cost?

- **Adequate Logging** – Do you have adequate logging turned ON to help in investigation if a breach happens?

You will be able to have a much better sleep if answers to the above questions are comforting to you.

ACTION PLAN AND CHECK MARKS

- **Fill the Gaps** – Fill any gaps that you find as a result of questions mentioned above. Document gaps with target dates to close the gaps in the action plan.

- **IR Partner** – Get an investigative response vendor contract who can make investigative resources available at a short notice. You will need help if a breach happens to continue normal operations as well as respond to the breach. This will comfort your business leaders as well as lower insurance cost.

- **Insurance Policy** – Data breach costs can reach many millions of dollars. An insurance policy helps in covering the cost.

- **Test IR Plan** – Test incident response plans regularly and make this testing part of security operations.

- **New Way of Thinking** – Update security monitoring processes assuming attackers have already breached into some parts of the network in your organization. Emphasize on detection mechanism.

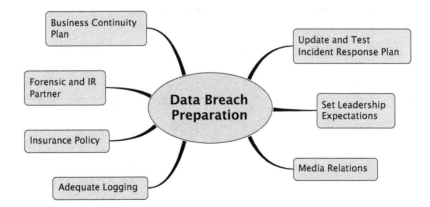

GOALS AND ACTIVITY LOG

Plan and record your activities related to the previous topic.

Date	Goal/Activity Description

29 Create Metrics for Essentials

In a previous chapter, we looked at a mind map showing a list of CISO responsibilities and a need to prioritize. While prioritizing, there is need to identify the minimum controls and technologies **essential** for the information security program. Every organization must implement these *essentials* to provide a baseline security program. The following mind map shows these *essentials* and relevant technologies in four areas.

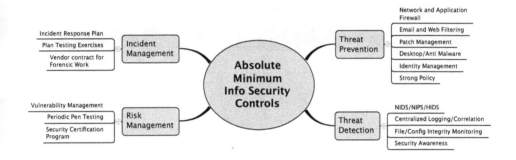

- **Determine Effectiveness** – The information security managers should create a metric to evaluate the effectiveness of the program in these areas.

- **Implementation is Important** – It matters less "*which*" technology is implemented compared to "*how*" it is implemented, managed, and monitored. An organization may have purchased the best tools but if these tools are not properly implemented and managed, you will not reap the benefits.

- **Expensive is not necessarily better** – There is no need to spend a fortune on essential tools and technologies. On my blog page, I compiled a list of open source/free tools that you can use. Visit http://rafeeqrehman.com/affordable-information-security/ to see the list of these tools.

Action Items

- **Implementation State** – Create a metrics that shows the current implementation status of solution in each of these areas. The implementation status may be (a) Fully implemented (b) Partially implemented (c) Not implemented.

- **Measure Effectiveness** – For fully and partially implemented solutions, the metrics should estimate the "*effectiveness*" of implementation.

- **Quarterly Progress** – Assign scores to each status and measure progress on a quarterly basis.

- A sample metrics may look like the following. Change and modify it to meet needs of your organization.

Security Essentials Score Card

Technology	Implementation	Software/Policy Updates	Centralized Log Integration	Monitoring	Score
Firewall	Fully Implemented	Yes	Yes	Yes	100
Web Filtering	Fully Implemented	Partial	No	Yes	50
Anti Malware	Partially Implemented	Yes	No	No	33

Overall Score: 61

GOALS AND ACTIVITY LOG

Plan and record your activities related to the previous topic.

Date	Goal/Activity Description

30 Measure ROSI

ROSI or Return On Security Investment is simply a way to calculate if a security control is worth implementation or not. For a control to be financially viable, the reduction of risk has to be greater than the cost of implementing security control.

In a very simplistic way, to calculate ROSI, you will calculate monetary risk for a specific incident and subtract the cost of implementing a security control to mitigate the risk. A positive value shows ROSI and the value of security control. A negative value indicates that the control is not worth implementation from a cost-benefit perspective.

ROSI = Reduction in Risk – Cost of Security Control

- **ROSI Calculators** – There are a number of online resources and calculators to measure ROSI and you can select one that you like. Searching on "ROSI Calculator" on the Internet will give you a number of links.

- **Simplicity** – Find a calculator that is simple as ROSI calculations can be very complicated depending upon how granular you want to go. I prefer simplicity at least in the initial phases.

- **ISACA published ROSI calculations guidelines** – These guidelines are available online and can be a good reference to start with. The guidelines are available under guideline number G41 on ISACA web site.

- **ROSI and Risk Calculations** – ROSI is tied to quantitative risk assessment. If your organization is not mature to perform quantitative risk calculations, calculation of ROSI may be tricky but not impossible.

Action Items

1. **Selective Use** – ROSI should be used only for *major* investments in information security. Avoid excessive use to ROSI calculators to save time.

2. **Business Justification Tool** – ROSI provides business justification of information security projects. Use it in project plans. It provides credibility of investments in information security.

3. Rationalize the calculations and share data with your executive team.

GOALS AND ACTIVITY LOG

Plan and record your activities related to the previous topic.

Date	Goal/Activity Description

31 Implement a Security Certification Program

Fixing problems in production systems is difficult and costly. The better way is to catch and fix security issues in design, implementation, and testing phases of system development lifecycle (SDLC).

- **Secure By Design** – A security certification program enables organizations to make security part of SDLC and ensure security is built into any new system as part of the project instead of an after thought.

- **Essential Part of SDLC** – Security certification program has to be an integral part of SDLC.

- **Gate Process** – Security certification can be included in gate processes when projects move from one phase to the next. A project moves to the next phase only when it has met security requirements.

- **Cost Saving** – Effective certification programs save cost and avoid delaying projects by avoiding identification of security issues at later stages.

Action Items

- **Certification and SDLC** – Identify owners of SDLC process in the organization and ensure that security is part of the lifecycle at least in the following stages:
  - **Requirements Phase** – Information security requirements and standards need to be part of the overall requirements. Examples include identity management, use of encryption, OWASP top 10, etc.
  - **Design Phase** – A security consultant must ensure all security requirements are incorporated in the system/software design.
  - **Implementation and Testing** – Security tools must be used to test the new system for any security flaws and to verify that security requirements are implemented properly.

- **Accreditation** – If any security flaws can't be fixed within the project, business owners must sign off on these issues and accept risk before a system is handed over to production/operations.

- **Templates and Artifacts** – Create standard templates and processes for security requirements, standards, testing procedures, and certification reports.

GOALS AND ACTIVITY LOG

Plan and record your activities related to the previous topic.

Date	Goal/Activity Description

Part Four

Risk Management

32 Understanding Risk

Risk is defined in many ways by different people. Basically, risk is probability of loss in future and a measure of uncertainty.

- **Risk Definitions** – Some definitions of risk are as follows:
    - **Wikipedia** – "Risk is the potential that a chosen action or activity (including the choice of inaction) will lead to a loss (an undesirable outcome[9])".
    - **FAIR** – "Risk – The probable frequency and probable magnitude of future loss[10]".
    - **COSO** – "Risk is the possibility that an event will occur and adversely affect the achievement of objectives[11]."

- **Risk Profiles Are Different** – Every organization has a different risk profile that depends upon type of organization, size of the organization, industry sector, geo political situation, location, and many other factors. Organizations in one industry sector may have different risk profile based upon factors mentioned above. A global bank will have a different risk profile than a small regional bank.

- **Risk is Not Static** – Risk profile keeps on changing over time as circumstances change. That is why periodic risk assessment is needed and essential for managing an effective risk management program.

- **Risk Management is Not Risk Elimination** – No matter how much money an organization spends on risk management, it is never zero. The objective of risk management is to keep this risk at a certain manageable level and not to completely eliminate it.

---

[9] http://en.wikipedia.org/wiki/Risk

[10] http://fairwiki.riskmanagementinsight.com/?page_id=6

[11] COSO, Enterprise Risk Management – Integrated Framework, September 2004, page 16.

- **Dealing With Risk** – While managing risk, organization's leadership team can decide to mitigate, transfer, or assume risk.

RECOMMENDED ACTIONS

- **Risk Education and Awareness** – Many people don't understand risk and that risk profiles continuously change. Make risk awareness as part of your education and awareness program.

- **Periodic Risk Assessment** – As mentioned in other parts of this book, make periodic risk assessment as part of information security program.

- **Chose Risk Assessment and Management Framework** – Select one of many risk assessment methodologies and a risk management framework. There is no silver bullet method and you can pick and chose different frameworks based upon your circumstances and maturity of your organization.

GOALS AND ACTIVITY LOG

Plan and record your activities related to the previous topic.

Date	Goal/Activity Description

33 Risk Drives Information Security Program

You can think of risk as a measure of likelihood of an incident and its impact on business. Everything an information security program does must be targeted towards reducing overall risk for the organization and be driven by periodic and formal risk assessments. If you have not done a formal risk assessment of your organization yet, *you may be trying to solve problems that don't exist* or have very low return on security investment or you may be overlooking things that really matter. Risk assessment will help picking in right type of projects in the following areas:

1. **Threat Prevention** – Firewalls, access controls, network segmentation, IPS, Security Policy, Awareness Program

2. **Threat Detection** – Log analysis, detection, alerting and monitoring

3. **Incident Management** – Incident response, forensics

A formal risk analysis will help in discovering gaps and in picking the right projects and security controls. It will provide a basis for information security operations. It will also be helpful for executives in your organization to understand why you do what you do. Risk analysis needs to be at the center of any information security program.

SUGGESTED ACTION ITEMS

To make risk analysis as part of your information security program, take following actions.

- **Qualitative or Quantitative** – Determine if you need to a qualitative or quantitative risk analysis. In most cases, qualitative risk analysis should be good enough. Only mature organization may opt for quantitative risk assessment.

- **Select a Framework and Methodology** – Select a risk assessment methodology that is suitable for your organization. Multiple methodologies exist and are being used in industry.

- **Set a formal risk assessment frequency**, that could be once or twice a year, and make it part of corporate policy.

- Use results of risk assessment as business justification for security projects.

- Make risk assessment as part of project delivery lifecycle in your organization (e.g. security certification program).

You may not be able to do all of these actions immediately. If that is the case, use an incremental approach and make them part of your information security roadmap.

GOALS AND ACTIVITY LOG

Plan and record your activities related to the previous topic.

Date	Goal/Activity Description

34 Asset Centric Approach

The biggest assets that any information security program is chartered to protect is the corporate data, intellectual property, and corporate reputation. The corporate reputation is essentially linked to protection of corporate data. To make data at the center of security operations, consider the following basics:

- **Location** – Where is the data located within your organization? Data discovery tools can help identify it.

- **Data Type and Sensitivity** – Data classification helps in understanding risk associated with the data.

- **Policy and Procedures** – After locating and classifying data, policies and procedures help protect that data.

- **Access Control** – Access controls enable an organization to provide access to data based upon need to know. An identity management program is essential for effective access control.

- **Alerting** – Unauthorized access needs to be monitored and alerted upon.

- **DLP** – Data Leakage Protection (DLP) enables organizations to monitor and alert on sensitive data leaving an organization.

While there are other non-tangible assets (e.g. reputation), data is the most important asset and criminals are after the data for financial benefits.

SUGGESTED ACTIONS

Following is an essential part of security operations. Create tasks/controls for an ongoing effort to discover data.

- **Data Discovery** – Users will store data at new locations. Data discovery has to be an ongoing or periodic process. It can be accomplished through biannual or annual controls.

- **Classification** – Data classification policy and procedures are required to understand importance of data.

- **RBAC** – Implement role based access controls (RBAC). Leverage LDAP, Active Directory or any other available user repository to implement RBAC. If current technologies don't allow implementation of RBAC, put this on information security roadmap.

- **DLP** – Data leakage prevention and detection should be part of strategy. Simple to complicated solutions are available for DLP.

- **Encryption** – Depending upon policy, encrypt data while stored, and while in transmission. There are multiple ways to *transparently* encrypt data without any action from users of the data.

- **Partner Access** – Implement specific access control for partners. Ensure proper language about data protection is included in contracts with partners who have access to data. Partners should agree to same standard of data classification/protection as your own organization.

Please see the following diagram to protect data as part of information security operations.

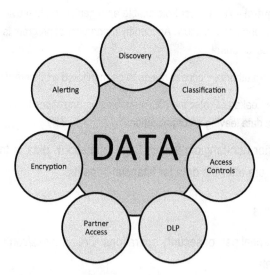

GOALS AND ACTIVITY LOG

Plan and record your activities related to the previous topic.

Date	Goal/Activity Description

35 Risk Management is Shared Responsibility

An effective risk management approach involves all areas of an organizational structure. It is a culture that involves collaboration, partnership, and awareness. You can think of it as moving parts of a machine. If one gear fails, it affects the whole operation.

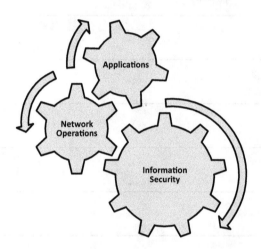

The CISO is like captain of a ship whose responsibility is to navigate through safe waters and stay away from rocks and storms. But all other crew members have a role in the safety of the ship, even the passengers. The captain can't save the ships if others are digging holes in the bottom.

An important part of a CISO role is to bring all areas together and ensure that:

- **Shred Responsibility** – People understand that risk management is a not the job of CISO or security team only. Everybody is a stakeholder in it.

- **Education and Awareness** – Build risk management and information security into the culture of an organization through education and awareness.

- **Executive Sponsorship** – Ensure that executive leadership fully stands behind and sponsors risk management program.

Risk management becomes quite effective when everyone takes an active role in the risk management under the guidance of CISO and the information security team.

SUGGESTED ACTIONS

Following are some actions you can take

- **Awareness Program** – Create an effective security and risk awareness program.

- **Find Common Objectives** – As mentioned in other parts of this book, build partnerships and find common grounds where risk management becomes a win-win situation for all stake holders.

- **Information Sharing** – Sharing information is better than not sharing. Some security teams are very closed; change this culture.

- **Don't be the boss** – In a shared culture, the security team should not act as a boss and dictate things. Justify the rationale of different security controls with logic to other IT teams.

GOALS AND ACTIVITY LOG

Plan and record your activities related to the previous topic.

Date	Goal/Activity Description

36 Risk Management Frameworks

Since risk is the basis of most of information security strategy and decision-making, a defined risk management framework is absolutely necessary for consistency in decision making process.

Risk management consists of multiple phases including the following. Remember risk assessment is subset of overall risk management framework.

- Risk identification

- Risk analysis and assessment

- Risk treatment

- Risk acceptance

- Risk communication

Commonly used risk frameworks are listed below. The objective of this book is not to describe these frameworks or provide a comparison but to get the reader started about picking a specific framework based upon their own assessment and circumstances. Readers can find comparison of these frameworks on multiple web sites and blogs.

- **NIST SP800-30** – http://csrc.nist.gov/publications/nistpubs/800-30/sp800-30.pdf

- **COSO** – http://www.coso.org

- **ISO/IEC** 31000 and ISO/IEC 27001/27005 – Principles and guidelines for risk management. I recommend reviewing all three at minimum starting with http://www.27000.org/iso-27001.htm

- **Octave** – Risk management methodology from CERT at http://www.cert.org/octave/

- **RiskIT** – RiskIT is part of COBIT 5 framework from ISACA

- **FAIR** – http://fairwiki.riskmanagementinsight.com or
  http://www.cxoware.com/software/fair-framework/

There are other frameworks like ISF, BASIL III (for banking/financials) that can be considered depending upon industry sector. Different government agencies have their own risk assessment frameworks.

SUGGESTED ACTIONS

- **Compare** – Make some time to evaluate different methods and review comparisons made by others.

- **Select** – Select one methodology and adapt it to your organization. Keep it simple, really simple.

- **Communicate** – Communicate the methodology to extended IT teams and the rationale for choosing it. Arrange lunch-n-learn sessions within your organization and get feedback. The objective is to ensure that people around you know which methodology you use and how it impacts IT.

- **Create a baseline** of current status of information security.

- **Create metrics** to measure progress.

GOALS AND ACTIVITY LOG

Plan and record your activities related to the previous topic.

Date	Goal/Activity Description

37 Controls Framework and Best Practices

Adoption of a comprehensive controls framework and set of best practices is necessary to run a measurable and predictable information security program. The controls framework must include preventive, detective, and corrective controls in functional areas such as physical, technology, processes, people, and compliance.

An organization can create a customized controls framework or adopt one of the major controls frameworks created by other vendors/organizations. In many cases, you may have multiple controls frameworks for different environments.

- **SANS top 20 critical controls** – This controls framework is defined after collaboration of multiple organizations and CISOs. It is available at http://www.sans.org/critical-security-controls/

- **Cloud Controls Matrix from Cloud Security Alliance (CSA)** – If you have or planning to have a cloud computing environment, CSA framework is a good place to look at - https://cloudsecurityalliance.org/research/ccm/

- **OWASP Top Ten** – OWASP top ten project is about most critical defects in web applications. This is a set of most common vulnerabilities and best practices to avoid these defects. Latest information about OWASP Top Ten is available at https://www.owasp.org/index.php/Category:OWASP_Top_Ten_Project

- **COBIT 5** – COBIT is an IT governance framework from ISACA and included recommendations and controls for information security.

- **ISO/IEC 27001** – Many organizations follow ISO standard controls.

- **NIST SP800-30** – NIST SP800-30 provides recommendations and controls for government organizations.

A number of government agencies around the world have also published their standardized controls frameworks. Adoption of specific controls will depend upon risk factors, type of business, legal, regulatory, and compliance requirements.

SUGGESTED ACTIONS

- **Needs Analysis** – Before adopting a controls framework, analysis of risk posture, compliance needs, and legal requirements is necessary.

- **Framework Analysis** – After assessing needs, an analysis of available frameworks should be done for suitability purposes. Existing frameworks are always a good start. If you are responsible for information security in a government agency, a framework may already be mandated by the government.

- **Start Small, Be Realistic** – While implementing information security frameworks, it may take some time to achieve maturity and comply with the framework. Set smaller goals and create a roadmap for next three years.

- **Assignment and Tracking** – Assign controls to specific persons and implement a progress tracking mechanism.

- **Incentives and Penalties** – Ensure that responsible parties fulfill controls by specific target dates by creating incentives and penalties.

GOALS AND ACTIVITY LOG

Plan and record your activities related to the previous topic.

Date	Goal/Activity Description

Part Five

Personal Branding

38 Create Your Brand and Market Yourself

Significant part of information security is related to credibility of CISO, psychology, and the confidence of business executives in ability of information security team to protect corporate information assets. A CISO has to make a conscious to create his/her brand, market himself/herself as well the information security team.

- Remember if you don't brand yourself, someone else will.
- Branding should be focused to both internal and external audience.
- A good brand will help you be more effective, make getting funding easy for security projects, and earn you respect.

Action Items

Here are some of the things you can do to build your own brand:

- **Write a blog on regular basis**. If you have an internal blog system, write a weekly blog for internal audience.
- **Use LinkedIn effectively**, show accomplishments instead of number of years of experience, use third person language on your profile.
- **Be technology savvy**, link your Twitter and Blog to LinkedIn. Tweet about things that matter in your field. Focus on your business in addition to information security.
- **Publish** your presentations at Slideshare
- **Speak** at conferences and local groups.
- Use some web sites or online tools to help promote your brand (e.g. Brandyourself.com)
- **Buy domain names** containing your names. You may need them in future or at least ensure no one else uses your name on web sites.

39 Know Commonly Used Technologies, Frameworks, and Standards

People respect knowledge. A high-level knowledge of commonly used technologies and standards is critical to success of information security professionals at all levels. If you are in a leadership role, it becomes even more critical to understand industry standards, technology, and the processes. Remember you don't need to know implementation details all the time but must have an understanding about how the technology works. For example, you don't need to be a DBA but need to know basics of databases to be an effective security professional. Many of these technologies are part of security certifications, however, the technology field is changing quickly and there is a need to keep oneself updated.

Following is a list of high-level technology areas that is very important to know for information security leaders.

- **ITIL** – Basics of ITIL including CMDB, ITSM, ITIL Foundation, Configuration Management, Change Control

- **Audit and Compliance** – SSAE 16, PCI, SOX, Privacy Laws, ISO 27K, HITRUST, HIPAA

- **Risk Management** – Frameworks and standards like ISO, COBIT, NIST, FAIR, Data sources like Verizon DBIR

- **Identity and Access Management** – Multi-factor authentication, SSO, SAML and Federation, PKI

- **Encryption** – Encrypting data at rest and in transit, desktop encryption options, key management, SSL, Email encryption

- **Fundamentals of databases** – CRUD, Data Warehouse, Normalization, Replication

- **Networking** – Basics of networking, IPv6, Tunneling, MPLS

- **Middleware** – Application Servers, Message Queues, Order Management

- **Project Management** – Critical Path, WBS, Gantt chart, deliverables

- **Applications** – High level idea about CRM, HRIS, FMIS, Payroll

- **Cloud** – Public/Private/Hybrid Clouds, IaaS, PaaS, SaaS

- **Application Development** – Frameworks like J2EE, Microsoft .Net, major vulnerabilities like OWASP top 10, SDLC

- **Architecture Standards** – TOGAF etc.

SUGGESTED ACTIONS

- **Learning TODO List** – Create a list of technologies that you need to learn.

- **Target Dates** – Use the following table to put target dates and measure your progress.

- **Online Courses** – Take free online courses using web sites like Coursera.

GOALS AND ACTIVITY LOG

Plan and record your activities related to the previous topic.

Date	Goal/Activity Description

40 Be a Relentless Seller

As a CISO (or other security leaders), many times you will find that your role is more of a Chief Information Security Seller. This is difficult role as you are selling something that does not have a tangible business outcome, or is at least many people have hard time to understand it. Continuous and relentless selling of information security causes is the only way to get funding for your projects.

- You have to sell information security causes internal to your organization as well as outside.

- It takes time for many people to **grasp the notion of risk**, so create and seek opportunities to convey your message in simple words.

- Speak at conferences on relevant topics.

- Use technologies like twitter, blogs, LinkedIn. Publish with online magazines.

- **Simplify Your Message** – Abstract messages are difficult to understand. Putting a picture in front of people helps a lot.

- **Value** – Like any other product or service, while selling security, focus on value proposition of security.

Action Items

- Create a **single slide security strategy** that you can show over and over.

- Seek opportunity for your internal monthly or quarterly meetings and provide updates on security landscape and how it impacts your organization.

- Publish an internal blog on weekly basis.

- Show numbers about how investment in security is benefiting your organization.

- **Seek partnerships** with network, application, operations, and database peers. Initiate projects that help more than one area of your business. Partner with PMO in SDLC, be part of change management initiatives.

- Help others achieve their goals and objectives, they will help you achieve yours.

- **Use of Graphical Tools** – Use graphical tools and rely less on Power Point presentations.

Goals and Activity Log

Plan and record your activities related to the previous topic.

Date	Goal/Activity Description

41 Use News and Media for Marketing and Awareness

The chances are that business executives in your organizations are fed stories by the news media about security breaches. So don't wait for an email from your CEO asking about a news story about a data breach in another corporation in your industry with questions like "what are we doing about it"? Instead, use news stories to your advantage and to promote information security agenda.

- Even if a news story is hype, people pay attention to it. *If it is in the news, it must be true.*

- Your executives may have rejected a budget proposal in the past to protect Personal Identifiable Information (PII). A news story about data breach involving email addresses may revive your project. Don't miss the chance! **Many times an incident elevates the risk very quickly** and turns the light bulbs on.

- **Inform leadership about relevant news** stories but always put a context to the story. Explain what it means to your organization (don't send an email with a URL only).

- Explain if the exploited weakness is already covered by existing controls or if there is a gap that needs to be plugged.

- Avoid too many emails to executives with news stories.

Effective use of news and media will help you create greater awareness, get budget approvals for security initiatives, and build your repute as someone who is on the top of current event.

TODO Items

- **Be a 15 minutes morning person**. Subscribe to important news outlets using RSS, browser reading list or any other technology at your disposal.

- **Follow important people** and security companies on Twitter.

- Write an internal memo about how a data breach may affect your organization, including direct and indirect costs. Indirect costs may include loss of reputation, wasted time in incident response, etc. Provide references to costs incurred by other organizations as result of data breaches.

- If there is a regular leadership meeting, use this meeting to **bring your leadership up to speed about relevant security events**, new regulations/laws or other relevant information. Create a recurring 15-minute segment in the leadership meetings on monthly basis.

GOALS AND ACTIVITY LOG

Plan and record your activities related to the previous topic.

Date	Goal/Activity Description

42 Join (or Start) Local CISO Forum

Ideas get refined when discussions happen. Everybody needs people who can listen, critique, and suggest improvements to the ideas and thoughts. Local CISO groups connect you with these people, and build a community around you. You will get good advice as well as help when you need it the most. With local CISO groups, you will be able to do things like:

- What works, or does not work.

- What mistakes others have already made, or pitfalls to avoid.

- Bring credibility to your work.

- Get to know industry trends and real life experiences.

Right kind of audience is important. The CISO group must be selective in granting membership. Invitation-only groups are even better.

Action Items

- Find a local group in your area and join it. If no group exists, start one.

- Make sure members of the group are thought leaders and bring value to other group members.

- Call quarterly meetings and create agenda for these meetings. Select a hot topic that may interest everyone. Invite speakers who may be members of this group.

- Ask you vendors to sponsor these meetings. Free food does have attraction!

GOALS AND ACTIVITY LOG

Plan and record your activities related to the previous topic.

Date	Goal/Activity Description

43 Learn Effective Public Speaking Skills

All great leaders, especially in technology, are known by great speeches and presentation. It is one of the most important personality traits to boost your personal brand and distinguish from others. You will often find reference to great speeches and presentations from technology leaders on LinkedIn, TED or other places. People just revere great presenters and try to follow them. And what is the most important thing a leader needs? Followers!

I am sure you always find yourself presenting solutions, new ideas, project plans, and budget requests to your peers and business leaders. Effective public speaking and presentation skills are key to success in any leadership role and CISO is no exception to it.

- Great presentations that create a "*vow effect*" will help you get your projects and budgets approved.

- You will build high **credibility** and great **respect** from your peers, higher ups, and people working for you.

- After your presentations, people will talk about you and will ask you to come and speak in their events, internal meetings, and conferences. This is a single best way to progress in your career.

Action Items

- There are many books but I recommend buying one particular book: The Exceptional Presenter.

- Write your presentation's major points and rehearse.

- **Record and watch** yourself doing presentation. These days it is very easy to use iPhone, Android or other hand held devices to record your audio and video.

- Review some of the tips from my previous blog post at http://rafeeqrehman.com/2012/04/23/leadership-getting-ready-for-a-great-presentation/

- Master the art of creating one-slide presentation.

GOALS AND ACTIVITY LOG

Plan and record your activities related to the previous topic.

Date	Goal/Activity Description

Part Six

Appendices

44 Appendix A: Web Site References

References

- CSO Online http://csoonline.com

- Leadership - http://www.forbes.com/leadership/

- OWASP top ten web application security risks - https://www.owasp.org/index.php/Top_10

- Safecode - http://www.safecode.org/publications/SAFECode_Dev_Practices0211.pdf

- OWASP Cheetsheets - https://www.owasp.org/index.php/Cheat_Sheets

- PII - http://en.wikipedia.org/wiki/Personally_identifiable_information

- ROSI – Is it possible to calculate ROSI? http://blog.iso27001standard.com/2011/06/13/is-it-possible-to-calculate-the-return-on-security-investment-rosi/

- ROSI Calculator - http://services.nsw.gov.au/inside-dfs/information-communications-technology/publications/return-security-investment

- ROSI ISACA guidelines - http://www.isaca.org/Knowledge-Center/Standards/Documents/G41-ROSI-5Feb10.pdf

Risk Management

- NIST - http://csrc.nist.gov/publications/nistpubs/800-39/SP800-39-final.pdf

- http://csrc.nist.gov/publications/nistpubs/800-37-rev1/sp800-37-rev1-final.pdf

- http://csrc.nist.gov/publications/drafts/800-30-rev1/SP800-30-Rev1-ipd.pdf

SEC Filings Search

- http://edgar.sec.gov

- http://en.wikipedia.org/wiki/SEC_filing

Information Security News

- SC Magazine - http://www.scmagazine.com

- Search Security - http://searchsecurity.techtarget.com

- SANS Security Resources - http://www.sans.org/security-resources/

- Packet Storm - http://packetstormsecurity.org

- Dark Reading - http://www.darkreading.com

- Security Week - http://www.securityweek.com

- The Register - http://www.theregister.co.uk

- Security Focus – http://www.securityfocus.com

- SecuriTeam – http://www.securiteam.com

- Packet Storm Security – http://www.packetstormsecurity.com

- Bugtraq mailing lists

General References

- Prevention, Detection, Response -
  http://www.giac.org/paper/gsec/501/information-security-process-prevention-detection-response/101197